# Summary

Some officials of the Islamic Republic of Iran have recently renewed threats to close or exercise control over the Strait of Hormuz. Iran's threats appear to have been prompted by the likely imposition of new multilateral sanctions targeting Iran's economic lifeline—the export of oil and other energy products. In the past, Iranian leaders have made similar threats and comments when the country's oil exports have been threatened. However, as in the past, the prospect of a major disruption of maritime traffic in the Strait risks damaging Iranian interests. U.S. and allied military capabilities in the region remain formidable. This makes a prolonged outright closure of the Strait appear unlikely. Nevertheless, such threats can and do raise tensions in global energy markets and leave the United States and other global oil consumers to consider the risks of another potential conflict in the Middle East. This report explains Iranian threats to the Strait of Hormuz, and analyzes the implications of some scenarios for potential U.S. or international conflict with Iran. These scenarios include:

- Outright Closure. An outright closure of the Strait of Hormuz, a major artery of the global oil market, would be an unprecedented disruption of global oil supply and contribute to higher global oil prices. However, at present, this appears to be a low probability event. Were this to occur, it is not likely to be prolonged. It would likely trigger a military response from the United States and others, which could reach beyond simply reestablishing Strait transit. Iran would also alienate countries that currently oppose broader oil sanctions. Iran could become more likely to actually pursue this if few or no countries were willing to import its oil.

- Harassment and/or Infrastructure Damage. Iran could harass tanker traffic through the Strait through a range of measures without necessarily shutting down all traffic. This took place during the Iran-Iraq war in the 1980s. Also, critical energy production and export infrastructure could be damaged as a result of military action by Iran, the United States, or other actors. Harassment or infrastructure damage could contribute to lower exports of oil from the Persian Gulf, greater uncertainty around oil supply, higher shipping costs, and consequently higher oil prices. However, harassment also runs the risk of triggering a military response and alienating Iran's remaining oil customers.

- Continued Threats. Iranian officials could continue to make threatening statements without taking action. This could still raise energy market tensions and contribute to higher oil prices, though only to the degree that oil market participants take such threats seriously.

If an oil disruption does occur, the United States has the option of temporarily offsetting its effects through the release of oil from the Strategic Petroleum Reserve. Such action could be coordinated with other countries that hold strategic reserves, as was done with other members of the International Energy Agency after the disruption of Libyan crude supplies in 2011.

Iran's threats suggest to many experts that international and multilateral sanctions—and the prospect of additional sanctions—have begun to affect its political and strategic calculations. The threats have been coupled with a publicly announced agreement by Iran to resume talks with six countries on measures that would assure the international community that Iran's nuclear program is used for purely peaceful purposes. Some experts believe that the pressure on Iran's economy, and its agreement to renewed talks, provide the best opportunity in at least two years to reach agreement with Iran on curbing its nuclear program.

# Contents

# Figures

# Tables

# Appendixes

# Contacts

# Geopolitical Considerations

From December 2011 to January 2012, some Iranian government officials openly threatened to close the Strait of Hormuz, a major artery of the global oil market, if sanctions are imposed on Iran's oil exports. Iran's first Vice President Mohammad Reza Rahimi first stated that threat on December 28, 2011. Various Iranian naval and other commanders restated and in some cases changed the threat somewhat. For example, on January 3, 2012, the commander of Iran's regular army, Ataollah Salehi, warned the United States not to return the departing U.S.S. *John Stennis* aircraft carrier to the Gulf.[1] Perhaps recognizing the potential for conflict with superior U.S. forces, a few Iranian figures, including regular Navy commander Habibollah Sayyari, issued statements downplaying or softening the warnings and threats.[2] The Iranian threats were issued during "Velayat 90," naval exercises held from December 23, 2011, to January 2, 2012, which culminated with the test firing of Iran-made surface-to-surface missiles. Oil exports are critical to Iran, providing 76% of export earnings and 62% of government revenues.[3] Many experts see Iran's warnings as a reiteration of its long held position to defend these exports.

## Context and Possible Causes of Iran's Threats

Iran's threats occurred as it faced increasing likelihood that multilateral sanctions would be adopted that could reduce Iran's oil export earnings. Previously, United Nations and multilateral sanctions had sought to reduce Iran's ability to develop its nuclear program by undermining its ability to develop its energy sector—targeting investment and financial linkages—but not directly targeting Iran's ability to export oil.[4]

- Following a report by the International Atomic Energy Agency (IAEA) on November 8, 2011,[5] which presented information that Iran had researched nuclear weapons designs in the past, the United States, Britain, and Canada took additional steps to shut Iran out of the international banking system.

- Iran reacted by expelling the British Ambassador to Iran. Then, on November 29, 2011, a mob ransacked the British Embassy in Tehran with the widely reported support of Iran's internal security force, the Basij militia. That action led to the closure of the Iranian and British embassies in London and Tehran, respectively.

- These events occurred at the same time Congress was completing action on the FY2012 National Defense Authorization Act (P.L. 112-81), containing a provision to sanction foreign banks that do business with Iran's Central Bank. Iran's Central Bank is the prime conduit through which buyers pay Iran for oil. That bill was signed into law on December 31, 2011.

---

[1] J. David Goodman. "Iran Warns U.S. Aircraft Carrier Not to Return to Gulf and a Strategic Strait." *New York Times*, January 4, 2012.

[2] Ramin Mostafavi. "Iran Test-Fires Missiles in Gulf Exercise." *Reuters*, January 2, 2012.

[3] For fiscal year 2009/10. International Monetary Fund, *Staff Report for the 2011 Article IV Consultation -- Islamic Republic of Iran*, July 5, 2011, p. 28, http://www.imf.org/external/pubs/ft/scr/2011/cr11241.pdf.

[4] Import of Iranian oil into the United States has been prohibited by U.S. law since 1995, but measures to end or reduce imports in Europe and other major markets are new.

[5] *Implementation of the NPT Safeguards*, http://isis-online.org/uploads/isis-reports/documents/IAEA_Iran_8Nov2011.pdf.

---

- The attack on British diplomatic property caused the EU to consider an embargo on purchases of Iranian oil, which was agreed to by EU foreign ministers on January 23, 2012.

## The Strait of Hormuz

The Strait of Hormuz is the narrow waterway that forms the entrance to the Persian Gulf from the Gulf of Oman and ultimately the Arabian Sea. At its narrowest point it is 22 nautical miles wide and falls within Iranian and Omani territorial waters. There are two shipping lanes through the Strait, one in each direction. Each is two miles wide and they are separated by a two-mile buffer. See **Figure 1**.

## Figure 1. Persian Gulf and the Strait of Hormuz

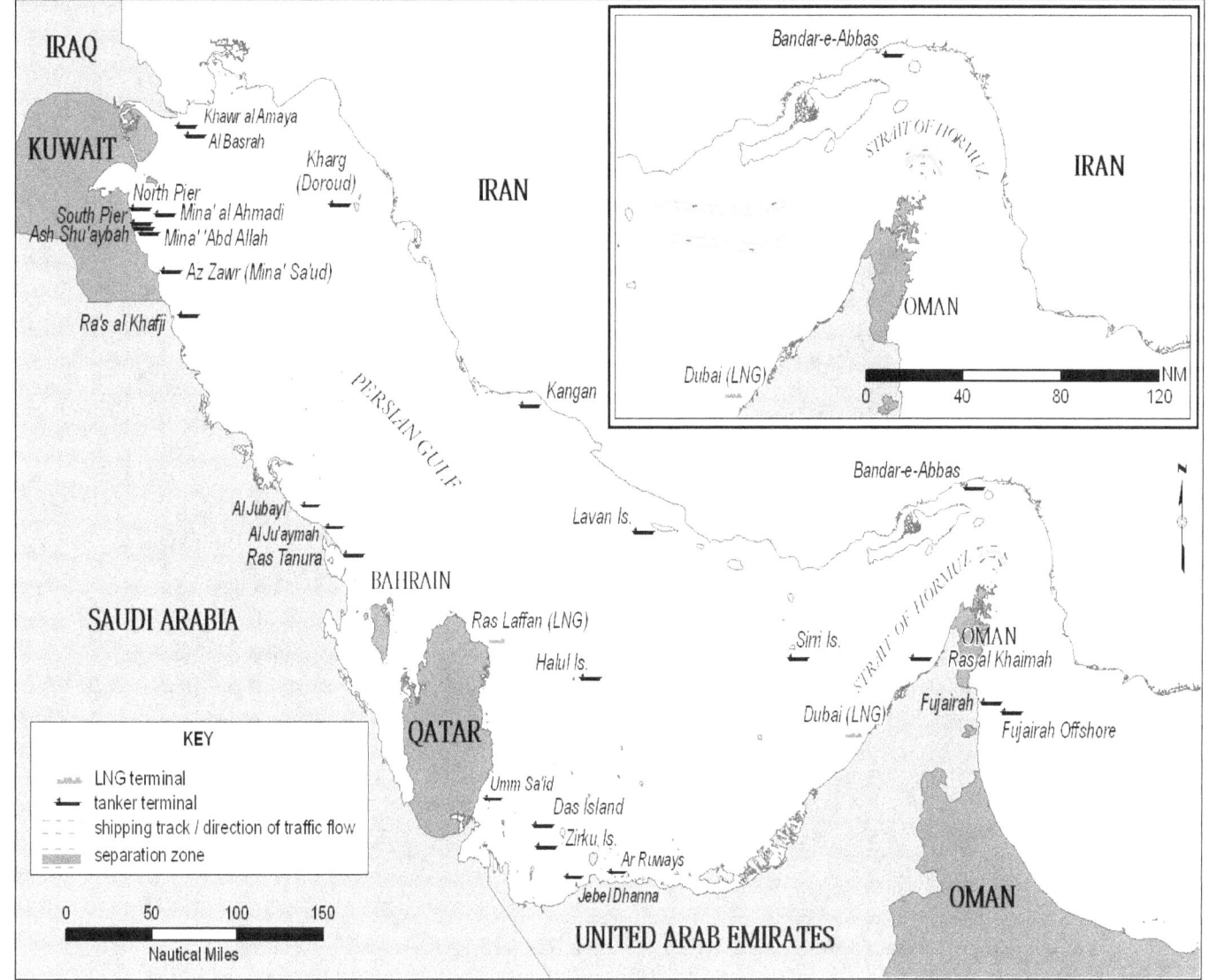

**Source:** Jacqueline Nolan, Library of Congress, with data from Petroleum Economist, National Oceanic and Atmospheric Administration, and Central Intelligence Agency.

## Iran's Intent to Implement Its Threats

Most observers believe that Iran, because of its own dependence on commerce through the Strait, intends to shape the international debate on Iran policy rather than to actually attempt to close the waterway. Oil exports are vital to the Iranian government's fiscal health and the Iranian economy as a whole. Iran relies on the Strait not only for its oil exports, but also for the shipment of some needed food and medical products, although Iran could attempt to re-route imports through ports outside the Strait, such as Jask, or with established overland trade routes through Pakistan or Iraq.

This implies that the likelihood that Iran might attempt to close the Strait increases if a broad embargo on purchases of Iran's oil emerges. At its January 23, 2012, meeting, the EU agreed to an embargo to take full effect by July 1, 2012. This EU move might remove what may be the most important factor restraining Iran from taking that step at this time. As a result of the EU decision, some Iranian leaders immediately reiterated the threat to the Strait. Some others threatened to immediately cut off exports to the EU and thereby deny the EU time to identify alternative suppliers.

Iran also may fear—and U.S. statements and actions seem to justify such a fear—that closing the waterway would provoke all-out conflict with the United States (see "U.S. Statements of Intent" below). Iran might be concerned that such a conflict would lead to U.S. military action not just to reopen the Strait but also to destroy its military and nuclear infrastructure.

Further, by threatening traffic through the Straits, Iran may risk alienating other nations, including its neighbors and customers. Most of the oil from the Persian Gulf goes to Asian nations. China is Iran's largest customer and Iran is China's third largest source of oil imports. In the wake of threats from Iran, China quickly dispatched Vice Foreign Minister Zhai Jun to Tehran, presumably to try to persuade Iran to withdraw its threats.[6] Chinese and Indian officials have indicated their countries will continue to buy Iranian crude.[7] However, according to reports, difficulties with payment terms have led to a reduction in Chinese import of Iranian crude in early 2012.[8]

## Iran's Capabilities to Implement Its Threat

In assessing Iran's capabilities to close the Strait, Chairman of the Joint Chiefs of Staff Martin Dempsey said on January 8, 2012, that:

> [The Iranians have] invested in capabilities that could, in fact, for a period of time block the Straits of Hormuz. We've invested in capabilities to ensure that, if that happens, we can defeat that. And so the simple answer is, yes, they can block it.[9]

Iran's naval capabilities are divided among the two main branches of its armed forces – the regular Islamic Republic of Iran Navy (IRIN, regular Navy), a holdover of the military of the

---

[6] Michael Singh, *The Real Iranian Threat in the Gulf*, January 3, 2012, http://www.washingtoninstitute.org/templateC06.php?CID=1789.

[7] Mari Iwata, "Japan Urges U.S. to Include China, India in Iran Sanctions," *Wall Street Journal*, January 18, 2012.

[8] Chen Aizhu, "China extends Iran oil import cut as sanctions mount," January 5, 2012.

[9] Comments by Joint Chiefs Chairman Dempsey on CBS TV program "Face the Nation," January 8, 2012.

---

former Shah of Iran, and the Islamic Revolutionary Guard Corps Navy (IRGC Navy). The IRIN controls the larger coastal combatant ships such as six Corvette-class (i.e., light frigate) ships. It also operates Iran's three Kilo-class submarines purchased in the 1990s from Russia. The more politically powerful IRGC Navy is a branch of the IRGC, which is considered allied to Iran's hardliners and which plays a role in internal security and support for pro-Iranian movements in the Middle East. The IRIN, with its larger ships, has been assigned to patrol the more open waters of the Gulf of Oman; the IRGC Navy, with its lighter fleet, is assigned to close-in waters of the Strait of Hormuz and Persian Gulf. As a hallmark of its role as guardian of the Islamic revolution, the IRGC Navy has long been perceived as more willing to undertake operations not fully vetted by senior political leaders, whereas the IRIN is considered more traditional and restrained in its approach.

Through new purchases and tactics adopted since the 1980-1988 Iran-Iraq war, Iran's naval forces have developed a clear asymmetric warfare capability intended to use Iran's long coast to frustrate larger adversaries. Among other specific capabilities in Iran's inventory are:[10]

- *Mines.* Iran is believed to possess as many as 5,000 mines of different types, including moored mines, advanced mines such as the MDM-3 that can be dropped from aircraft, and other types.[11] Detecting and clearing mines once they have been placed in the water can be difficult and time-consuming task. Mine-clearing operations could be made more challenging if they are undertaken while U.S. and coalition forces are also attempting to counter other Iranian forces, such as speed boats, mini-submarines, and shore-based cruise missiles. U.S. and coalition forces might choose to suppress other threats before starting mine-clearing operations. This could reduce the risk to mine-clearing forces, but lengthen the total timeline for clearing the Gulf of mines.

- *Small Boats.* The IRGC Navy is perceived as a greater threat for "asymmetric warfare" because of its small fleet and unconventional tactics, such as "swarming," which it has developed since the end of the Iran-Iraq war in 1988. Swarming is characterized by deployment of dozens, or perhaps even hundreds of cruise-missile or other armed small boats, launched from different bases, to converge on and attack a discreet target such as a warship or oil tanker.[12] Numerous U.S. observers are particularly concerned about the use of such tactics, particularly in the relatively close confines of the Strait of Hormuz.[13] To carry out

---

[10] Some of the capabilities in which Iran has invested are discussed in various military-related journals, such as "The Military Balance: 2011," published by the International Institute of Strategic Studies in Britain. Additional detail is provided in an unclassified study by the Office of Naval Intelligence, "Iran's Naval Forces: From Guerrilla Warfare to a Modern Naval Strategy," Fall 2009.

[11] Tony Capaccio, "Keeping Strait Open to Get Tougher as Iran Expands Forces," *Bloomberg News,* January 18, 2012.

[12] For more information, see Fariborz Haghshenass, "Iran's Doctrine of Asymmetric Naval Warfare," Washington Institute for Near East Policy, PolicyWatch 1179, December 21, 2006. http://www.washingtoninstitute.org/templateC05.php?CID=2548

[13] See, for example, Michael Rubin, "Dire Straits," *Weekly Standard,* January 16, 2012. One observer has taken an opposing view, stating:

> The IRGCN small-boat threat is largely unchanged [since the U.S.-Iranian naval clashes of the 1980s] and can be successfully countered.

> The IRGCN tactics and command-and-control abilities to execute small-boat attacks have not changed significantly. Iran has not displayed credible command-and-control to employ swarms of small boats effectively, other than in staged exercises, and the IRGCN does not usually deploy

(continued...)

---

this tactic, among others, the IRGC Navy controls a large number of generally smaller ships of many different classes. These include: 10 China-supplied Hudong-class missile patrol boats bought in the 1990s and equipped with C-802 sea-skimming cruise missiles; 9 C-14 missile boats, also made by China and received in 2006; another China-made boat, the MK-13 patrol craft that can be armed with cruise missiles and torpedoes; about 40 Iran-made patrol craft called the PEYKAAP; and 30-40 Swedish-made *Boghammer* fast-patrol boats. Iran also has an unspecified number of small boats designed in Italy (Fabio Buzzi Design) but made in Iran itself.

- *Submarines.* Torpedoes launched from Iran's three Kilo-class submarines or its up to nearly a dozen mini or midget submarines could inflict potentially devastating damage on a warship, as shown by the March 2010 sinking of the South Korean corvette *Cheonan* by a torpedo that South Korea, United States, and other countries concluded was fired by a North Korean mini-submarine. Iran's decision to base its three Russian-made Kilo-class submarines outside the Strait of Hormuz suggests that the ships would be used during a confrontation to threaten surface ships operating in the Gulf of Oman.

- *Coastal Cruise Missiles.* The IRGC Navy controls several batteries of CSS-C-2 "Seersucker" and China-made C-801 and C-802 anti-ship missiles emplaced along Iran's coast. These missiles can be readily deployed anywhere along the Iranian coast. Lebanese Hezbollah, which is supported and armed by Iran, used a C-802 to severely damage an Israeli naval vessel in the 2006 Israel-Hezbollah war.

## Scenarios for Long Term Low-Intensity Conflict in the Gulf

Rather than close the Strait outright, some experts believe that it is more likely that Iran would use the capabilities discussed to disrupt, threaten, harass, and otherwise create substantial instability for shipping in the Gulf. Similar to attempting to close the Strait, employing these low-intensity tactics and operations could be intended to cause the United States and its partners to think twice about increasing economic, diplomatic, or military pressure against Iran.

---

(...continued)

more than three to five boats together. The machine guns and rocket launchers deployed on its small-boat fleet remain highly inaccurate to hit anything but a lumbering, unmaneuverable supertanker.

In previous engagements, the U.S. military has dominated Iranian small boats. Even conventional combatants such as the cruiser Vincennes, in its firefight with Iranian small boats in July 1988, showed that the five-inch guns could strike IRGCN boats before they could get close enough to fire their rockets and machine guns. Naval Special Warfare Mark V and Special Operations Craft–Riverine (SOC–R) patrol boats, along with armed Coast Guard vessels, are more than a match for the IRGCN small boats. U.S. Special Warfare sailors are better trained and disciplined than IRGCN personnel. A firefight between small boats of these opposing forces would be a one-sided engagement.

(David B. Crist, *Gulf of Conflict: A History of U.S.-Iranian Confrontation at Sea*, Washington Institute for Near East Policy, June 2009 (Policy Focus #95), pp. 30-31.)

---

Iran might begin with a less violent option and progress over time to more violent ones, or implement a combination of highly violent options from the outset. Potential options available to Iran include but are not limited to the following, which are listed in no particular order:

- Declaring that the Strait of Hormuz or other parts of the Gulf are closed to shipping, without stating explicitly what the consequences might be for ships that attempt to transit those waters.

- Declaring more explicitly that ships transiting the Strait or other parts of the Gulf are subject to being intercepted and detained, or attacked.

- Using speed boats, other surface craft, or aircraft to harass, block the path of, or fire warning shots at ships transiting the Strait or other parts of the Gulf.

- Using the above assets, and perhaps also shore-based rockets, artillery, and cruise missiles, mini-submarines, or swimmers, to selectively or more systematically attack selected ships transiting the Strait or other parts of the Gulf.

- Mining the Strait and perhaps other parts of the Gulf.

- Declaring that foreign naval ships operating in certain waters outside the Strait (i.e., in the Gulf of Oman) will be subject to attack.

- Using submarines, surface ships, shore-based cruise missiles, and aircraft to attack foreign naval ships operating in waters outside the Strait.

In response to subsequent U.S. and coalition military actions to keep the Gulf open, Iran's list of potential options would expand to include using theater ballistic missiles, submarines, commandos, or aircraft to attack military or economic land targets on the western side of the Gulf, and perhaps ordering terrorist attacks against targets both in the Persian Gulf region and beyond.

There is precedent for many of the scenarios discussed above. Iran used many of these tactics during the 1980-1988 Iran-Iraq war in an effort to respond to Iraq's conventional air superiority and to the perceived U.S. alignment with Iraq in that war. Iran laid mines in the Gulf to disrupt tanker traffic and used Chinese-made Silkworm cruise missiles to damage oil tankers and oil loading facilities. These actions prompted U.S. operation Earnest Will (July 1987-September 1988), to reflag and militarily escort through the Gulf Kuwaiti oil tankers and to de-mine the Gulf. When a mine struck the U.S.S. *Samuel B. Roberts* on April 14, 1988, it prompted the U.S. to launch operation Praying Mantis (April 18, 1988), in which the U.S. Navy attacked two Iranian oil platforms. Iran attempted a retaliatory assault on U.S. naval forces in the Gulf which resulted in the destruction of about 25% of Iran's conventional naval fleet. Iran also had one failed attempt to use "swarming" tactics—that time against a fixed infrastructure target—in October 1987: Iran sent a flotilla of about 60 small boats to attack the Saudi-Kuwaiti offshore oil terminal at Khafji, but was turned back by Saudi Arabia's air force. The Saudis reportedly were alerted to the attack by the United States.

Later, in the mid-1990s, Iran raised substantial U.S. and Gulf state concerns by building up troops, artillery, cruise missiles, and anti-aircraft artillery on islands in the Gulf, including those it has seized from the United Arab Emirates.[14] More recently, in March 2007, Iran seized and held

---

[14] For a discussion of the crisis created by this buildup, see CRS Report 95-572, *Iranian Military Buildup: What Sort of Threat to Persian Gulf Oil Supply?* by Lawrence C. Kumins and Kenneth Katzman, May 1, 1995 (out of print; (continued...)

for about two weeks a group of British marines whose ship Iran said had wandered into its territorial waters—an assertion denied by Britain.

# Potential Diplomatic Resolution of the Iranian Threat

Resumed multilateral nuclear talks could provide a diplomatic means to reduce any threat Iran posed to traffic through the Strait. Since 2006, Iran has negotiated with six countries—the so-called "P5+1," permanent U.N. Security Council members plus Germany—to identify steps that could assure the international community that Iran's nuclear program is purely peaceful. The last round of talks was held in January 2011, and made virtually no progress, contributing to subsequent U.S. and EU decisions to add sanctions against Iran.

Recently, Iran has shown interest in resuming nuclear talks, perhaps in an attempt to head off broadening sanctions. On December 31, 2011, Iran's chief nuclear negotiator, Seyed Jallili, stated that Iran would respond positively to an October 2011 letter by EU foreign policy director Catherine Ashton to enter a new round of nuclear negotiation. However, and despite comments by Iranian President Mahmud Ahmadinejad on January 26, 2012 welcoming new talks, no formal response has been sent and no talks are scheduled. Progress on these talks could motivate the EU to weaken sanctions, which in turn could reduce Iran's motivation to threaten traffic through the Strait. As a further sign of conciliation, Iran allowed an International Atomic Energy Agency team to visit Iran to discuss Iran's past work on a nuclear explosive device. The visit occurred during January 29-31, 2012. These issues are discussed in greater detail in CRS Report RS20871, *Iran Sanctions*, by Kenneth Katzman.

# Potential Military Response

## U.S. Statements of Intent

U.S. officials have stated that the United States would not tolerate an attempt by Iran to close the Strait, and would respond by taking action to reopen the waterway:

- On December 28, 2011, a spokeswoman for the U.S. Navy's 5th Fleet, which is responsible for the Persian Gulf region, stated, "Anyone who threatens to disrupt freedom of navigation in an international strait is clearly outside the community of nations; any disruption will not be tolerated."[15] That same day, DOD press secretary George Little reportedly stated "Any attempt to close the strait will not be tolerated."[16]

- On January 8, 2012, in an interview on the CBS television show *Face The Nation*, Secretary of Defense Leon Panetta stated, "We have made very clear that the United States will not tolerate blocking of the Straits of Hormuz. That's

---

(...continued)

available from the author).

[15] Barbara Starr and Phil Gast, "U.S. Navy Won't Tolerate 'Disruption' Through Strait of Hormuz," *CNN.com*, December 29, 2011; Thomas Erdbrink, "Iran Seen As Unlikely To Close Hormuz Strait," *Washington Post*, December 29, 2011: 8; Mark Thompson, "Can Iran Close The Strait of Hormuz" *Battleland.Blogs.Time.com*, December 28, 2011.

[16] Farnaz Fassihi, "U.S. Warns Tehran On Strait," *Wall Street Journal*, December 29, 2011: 8.

another red line for us—and that we will respond to that." In the same interview, General Martin Dempsey, the Chairman of the Joint Chiefs of Staff, stated, that "we've described that as an intolerable act. And it's not just intolerable for us. It's intolerable to the world. But we would take action and reopen the straits."[17]

- On January 13, 2012, it was reported that "The Obama Administration is relying on a secret channel of communication to warn Iran's supreme leader, Ayatollah Ali Khamenei, that closing the Strait of Hormuz is a 'red line' that would provoke an American response...."[18]

Although U.S. statements have addressed Iran's threat to close the Strait outright, it is widely assumed by experts and observers that the United States will act against Iranian efforts to harass or interfere with the free flow of commerce in the Strait in such scenarios discussed above. As noted previously, the United States skirmished with Iran repeatedly during 1987-88 on occasions where Iran sought to interfere with international shipping but did not try to close the Strait outright.

## U.S. Confidence in Its Ability to Keep the Strait Open

There appears to be a general consensus among observers who track Iran's armed forces that Iran has the military capacity—using mines, speed boats, submarines, shore-based cruise missiles, aircraft and other systems—to disrupt the flow of commercial shipping into and out of the Persian Gulf. There also appears to be a consensus that the U.S. military, acting alone or with coalition partners, has the capacity to then counter Iran's forces and restore the flow of shipping, but that the effort would likely take some time—days, weeks, or perhaps months—particularly if a large number of Iranian mines needed to be cleared from the Gulf. However, U.S. forces are presumably monitoring for mine deployment and may interrupt such an initiative by Iran before a large number of mines were able to be deployed. This in turn runs the risk of leading to more extensive military engagement.

A January 13, 2012, press report stated, "Estimates by naval analysts of how long it could take for American forces to reopen the strait range from a day to several months, but the consensus is that while Iran's naval forces could inflict damage, they would ultimately be destroyed."[19] A January 5, 2012, press report states that "Should Iran's rulers ever make good their threats to block the Straits of Hormuz, they could almost certainly achieve their aim within a matter of hours. But they could also find themselves sparking a punishing—if perhaps short-lived—regional conflict from which they could emerge the primary losers.... Few believe Tehran could keep the straits closed for long—perhaps no more than a handful of days...."[20] A December 29, 2011, press report states that "Iran can disrupt traffic through the Strait of Hormuz but probably cannot completely shut down the world's most important oil route, military analysts say.... What the Iranians can do ... is harass traffic through the Gulf—anything from stopping tankers to outright attacks. The goal

---

[17] Source: Transcript of interview with Secretary Panetta and General Dempsey, Face The Nation (CBS), January 8, 2012. Panetta said this was "another" red line because earlier in the interview, he identified the development by Iran of a nuclear weapon as a red line.

[18] Elisabeth Bumiller, Eric Schmitt, and Thom Shanker, "U.S. Sends Top Iranian Leader a Warning on Strait Threat," *New York Times*, January 13, 2012: 1.

[19] Ibid.

[20] Peter Apps, "Iran Could Close Hormuz—But Not For Long," *Reuters.com*, January 5, 2012.

would be to panic markets, drive up shipping insurance rates and spark a rise in world oil prices enough to pressure the United States to back down on sanctions."[21]

An Iranian attempt to close the Gulf to shipping could take many forms, as could a U.S. and coalition military response. In a military confrontation between Iran and the United States and other countries over the flow of shipping into and out of the Gulf, events could unfold and culminate rapidly, within a few hours or days, or more slowly, over a period of weeks or months. There might be multiple rounds of Iranian initiatives and U.S. and coalition responses, with quieter periods in between. During these events, there might be few or no moments when the Gulf is fully closed (i.e., no ships entering or leaving) or fully open (i.e., ships entering or leaving with no risk of Iranian harassment or attack). The confrontation would carry a risk of escalating to a wider military conflict between Iran and the United States and coalition partners.

The possibility of conflict with Iran complicates U.S. defense policy just weeks after completing a U.S. troop pullout from Iraq and the announcement of a new defense guidance predicated on shrinking resources. The new guidance includes an increased emphasis on the Asia-Pacific region but also states that the U.S. military will invest in capabilities required to operate effectively against any moves by actors such as Iran or China to counter U.S. power-projection capabilities.

## Potential U.S. and Coalition Military Responses

It is possible that U.K. forces would join U.S. forces in responding militarily to an Iranian attempt to close the Gulf. The U.K.'s Secretary of Defense, Philip Hammond, stated in early January 2012

---

[21] Lee Keath, "Closing Strait A High Cost For Iran," *ArmyTimes.com*, December 29, 2011. See also Mark Thompson, "Can Iran Close The Strait of Hormuz" *Battleland.Blogs.Time.com*, December 28, 2011, which quotes a 2008 Naval War College study by Navy Commander Rodney Mills as stating:

> There is consensus among the analysts that the U.S. military would ultimately prevail over Iranian forces if Iran sought to close the strait. The various scenarios and assumptions used in the analyses produce a range of potential timelines for this action, from the optimistic assessment that the straits would be open in a few days to the more pessimistic assessment that it would take five weeks to three months to restore the full flow of maritime traffic.

A September 2011 report from CNA (Center for Naval Analyses) stated:

> A detailed analysis of this question was conducted by [Caitlin] Talmadge using a scenario in which Iran was able to lay several hundred mines in the Strait and the Persian Gulf. In her analysis, Talmadge assumes the U.S. considers its mine countermeasure (MCM) forces too vulnerable and scarce to use in a hostile environment, and so would instead wait to use them until it had essentially eliminated the threat from [antiship cruise missiles] ASCMs. Using a technical analysis of U.S. air and Iranian ASCM and air-defense capabilities, she concluded it could take between 9 and 72 days for the U.S. to do so. Using mine-clearance rates based on previous efforts in the Persian Gulf (e.g., Operation Candid Hammer), she concluded it would take between 28 and 40 days to adequately clear the minefields. Putting these two timelines together, she concluded overall that it could take 37 to 112 days for the U.S. to reopen the Strait under such a scenario. Many of her assumptions regarding Iranian capabilities were subsequently disputed as giving the Iranians too much credit, but the disputer did not rule out completely the capability of Iran to threaten the Strait.

> (Jonathan Schroden, *A Strait Comparison: Lessons Learned from the 1915 Dardanelles Campaign in the Context of a Strait of Hormuz Closure Event*, CNA (Center for Naval Analyses), September 2011, pp. 38-39. The analysis by Talmadge cited in the CNA report is: Caitlin Talmadge. "Closing Time: Assessing the Iranian Threat to the Strait of Hormuz," *International Security*, Summer 2008: 82-117. The CNA report cites the following source for the subsequent dispute over Talmadge's assumptions regarding Iranian capabilities: William D. O'Neil and Caitlin Talmadge. "Costs and Difficulties of Blocking the Strait of Hormuz," *International Security*, Winter 2008/09: 190-198.)

---

that "Disruption to the flow of oil through the Strait of Hormuz would threaten regional and global economic growth. Any attempt by Iran to do this would be illegal and unsuccessful."[22] Since that statement, Britain reportedly has sent additional warships to the Gulf to augment U.S. capabilities there.

Other potential coalition partners would include other western allies and the Gulf Cooperation Council states. Asian oil consumers have also signaled their discomfort with the prospect of disruption and could take a negative stance against any Iranian action to disrupt or close the Strait.

U.S. and coalition military actions would likely be tailored to a large degree on the exact nature of Iran's actions. U.S. and coalition forces could clear mines, organize convoys or establish a protected shipping corridor, and defend ships against Iranian attacks without attacking Iranian targets ashore. A broader alternative would be to extend operations to include air strikes against shore-based Iranian anti-ship weapons and supporting surface-to-air missile batteries, radars, and command-and-control facilities. A still-broader alternative would be to extend options further, to include strikes against shore-based Iranian military assets that are not involved in Iran's effort to close the Gulf, including, potentially, targets believed to be associated with the development of an Iranian nuclear weapon capability. U.S. and coalition forces could attack Iranian anti-shipping assets only after Iran has used them to attack ships, or attack those assets preemptively. Attacks could be concentrated against assets of the IRGC, which has primary responsibility for the Persian Gulf within Iran's military establishment, or be spread more broadly to also include assets of Iran's state armed forces.[23]

---

[22] James Blitz, "UK Warns Iran Over Hormuz Threat," *Financial Times*, January 5, 2012: 5. See also Thomas Harding, "Navy Sends Top Warship To Gulf As Iran Threatens To Block Key Oil Route," *London Daily Telegraph*, January 7, 2012, and Keith Johnson, "Threat By Iran Adds To Specter Of Conflict In Oil Lane," *Wall Street Journal*, January 7, 2012: 8.

[23] A 2009 study that reviewed U.S.-Iranian naval clashes in the Gulf in the 1980s stated:

> The United States must be prepared for robust retaliation should an asymmetrical attack in a future regional conflict escalate (or if the IRGCN decides to employ its missile boats) and a larger response becomes necessary. Such a response should come in the form of a series of targeting packages based upon graduated response options, ranging from IRGC targets only to more expansive attacks on Iran's military infrastructure.

> A key question with no historical precedent is how Iran would respond to an attack on its mainland, either in response to a provocation or to destroy its nuclear weapons capability. During Operation Earnest Will, CENTCOM developed a series of scaled military options. The commander, Gen. George Crist, recommended as a first option attacking targets that facilitated Iran's ability to sustain its operations in the Gulf. He proposed seizing one or all of the islands of Farsi, Sirri, or Abu Musa, as well as destroying the oil platforms Iran used to collect intelligence and command the IRGCN. In a memo for the chairman of the Joint Chiefs, the CENTCOM commander said he wanted to "deny their eyes and forward staging bases within the Gulf." Iran would then be forced to sortie from its mainland and "would be more susceptible to detection and interdiction than is now the situation where Gulf havens afford cover, concealment, and support." In keeping with this strategy, U.S. Army and Marines planned to seize the Iranian offshore oil platforms and the larger islands, Abu Musa and Farsi Island in particular, during Operation Earnest Will.

> If such a plan failed to deter Iran, CENTCOM planned to escalate and strike Iranian air and naval targets on the mainland. First on the target list were the Silkworm missile storage sites and Iranian intelligence sites. Other strike packages included Bandar Abbas (to destroy IRIN and IRGC forces). Fourteen B-52s with a mixed load, including precision-guided cruise missiles, would knock out the hard-to-reach targets, such as the Bandar Abbas air defense headquarters and the First Naval District Headquarters building, while others would attack the Bandar Abbas Naval Base. Simultaneously, U.S. Navy aircraft and F-16s based in Bahrain or Saudi Arabia would strike the air

(continued...)

---

As far as mine-clearing operations, during the 1980s tanker war in the Gulf, a total of 17 minesweepers (six from the U.S. Navy, nine from European navies, and two from the Soviet Navy)[24] were used to clear mines from the Gulf. Given the limited mine-clearing assets that the United States has stationed at Bahrain (four mine countermeasures ships and one squadron of mine-clearing helicopters[25]), the additional minesweepers provided by coalition partners could be of particular value in mitigating the need for the United States to transport additional mine-clearing ships and helicopters into the area.

U.S. and coalition forces could counter Iranian speed boats and surface craft operating at sea using ship-based guns and missiles as well as land- and sea-based airplanes and helicopters armed with missiles, rockets, guided bombs, and guns. U.S. and coalition naval forces could use aircraft to attack Iranian speed boats and other surface craft that are tied up at pier, but Iran could make this more difficult by dispersing its speed boats and other surface craft along Iran's lengthy Persian Gulf shoreline. U.S. and coalition military leaders might choose to initially keep their warships out of confined waters until the threat posed by speed boats has been suppressed by attacks from aircraft; doing so could reduce the risk to U.S. or coalition warships but lengthen timelines for reopening the Gulf.

Some of Iran's shore-based anti-ship cruise missiles (ASCMs) are fired from launchers that are mobile and camouflaged, making them more difficult to locate and destroy. Even so, a January 5, 2012, press report quoted a "U.S. naval officer with considerable experience in the region" as stating "Anti-ship cruise missiles are mobile, yet can ... be found and destroyed."[26] Many of the radars that provide targeting for these missiles reportedly are in fixed locations, making them easier to attack.[27]

With regard to combating Iran's submarine capabilities, detecting a well-maintained, proficiently operated Kilo-class submarine that is submerged and waiting quietly near a choke point like the Strait of Hormuz can be a challenge for a navy, even the U.S. Navy, that has capable antisubmarine forces. On the other hand, the threat posed by Kilo-class submarines can be reduced by tracking their movements in the days and weeks prior to the start of a confrontation. Diesel-electric submarines like the Kilo design have a submerged endurance of no more than a few days, and are vulnerable to attack when they surface to snorkel. They are also vulnerable in port.

Iran's mini-submarines are more likely to be used inside the Gulf. Their small size could make them particularly difficult to detect, but they also have limited at-sea endurance and can carry

---

(...continued)

defense headquarters and destroy Iranian surface-to-air Hawk missiles that ring Bandar Abbas airport, which, in addition to being a commercial airport, was the main southern airfield for IRIAF and its complement of F-4 fighters.

(David B. Crist, *Gulf of Conflict: A History of U.S.-Iranian Confrontation at Sea*, Washington Institute for Near East Policy, June 2009 (Policy Focus #95), p. 32.

[24] David B. Crist, *Gulf of Conflict: A History of U.S.-Iranian Confrontation at Sea*, Washington Institute for Near East Policy, June 2009 (Policy Focus #95), p. 31.

[25] Jonathan Schroden, *A Strait Comparison: Lessons Learned from the 1915 Dardanelles Campaign in the Context of a Strait of Hormuz Closure Event*, CNA (Center for Naval Analyses), September 2011, p. 43.

[26] Peter Apps, "Iran Could Close Hormuz—But Not For Long," *Reuters.com*, January 5, 2012. The ellipsis in the quote as in the article.

[27] Lee Keath, "Closing Strait A High Cost For Iran," *ArmyTimes.com*, December 29, 2011.

limited ordnance payloads. The naval officer cited above reportedly also said of Iran's forces that "Submarines are short-duration threats—they eventually have to come to port for resupply and when they do they will be sitting ducks."[28]

# Oil Market Considerations

The Strait of Hormuz is a key artery of the global oil market. Persian Gulf oil exporters—Iraq, Kuwait, Saudi Arabia, the United Arab Emirates and Qatar—shipped about 17 million barrels a day (Mb/d) of oil through the Strait in 2011, which is roughly 20% of the global oil market and 35% of seaborne trade according to the Energy Information Administration.[29] On average, 14 crude oil tankers leave the Persian Gulf through the Strait each day with more than 85% of these crude oil exports going to Asian countries, including China, Japan, India, and South Korea.[30] The United States imports 1.8 Mb/d from Persian Gulf countries, roughly 10% of U.S. consumption.[31] Separately, more than a quarter of the world's liquefied natural gas (LNG) trade, equal to about 2.6% of global natural gas consumption, moves through the Strait.[32] This is primarily exports from Qatar to Europe and Asia. The United States imports little LNG.

The Persian Gulf is also home to the world's spare oil production capacity. Current estimates for global spare oil production capacity tend to be around 2 to 3 Mb/d. OPEC members hold spare capacity as a result of their market management strategy.[33] Basically all of this spare capacity is held by Persian Gulf oil producers—mostly Saudi Arabia, with small amounts in Kuwait and the United Arab Emirates. Spare capacity is viewed as a cushion to the oil market which can be used to offset supply disruptions. However, given its location, this spare capacity would not be available to offset a disruption to the Strait of Hormuz.

There is little ability for oil shipments to bypass the Strait through alternative routes, particularly in the short-run. According to reports, Saudi Arabia could redirect 1.5 Mb/d of oil currently exported through the Persian Gulf to terminals on its Red Sea coast through unutilized capacity currently available on its East-West pipeline.[34] A 1.5 Mb/d pipeline to bypass the Strait is being built in the United Arab Emirates, but it is not likely to be completed until the middle of 2012.[35] Several other pipelines that ran through Iraq and Saudi Arabia to the Mediterranean and Red Sea export facilities have been out of operation for many years, and it is unclear how readily they could be returned to operation.

---

[28] Peter Apps, "Iran Could Close Hormuz—But Not For Long," *Reuters.com*, January 5, 2012.

[29] Energy Information Administration, U.S. Department of Energy, *The Strait of Hormuz is the world's most important oil transit chokepoint*, Today in Energy, January 4, 2012, http://www.eia.gov/todayinenergy/detail.cfm?id=4430#.

[30] Ibid.

[31] Average imports, January to October 2011. Much of U.S. import from the region likely come through the Strait. For more background on U.S. imports, see CRS Report R41765, *U.S. Oil Imports: Context and Considerations*, by Neelesh Nerurkar.

[32] Based on data from the BP Statistical Review of World Energy, http://www.bp.com/statisticalreview.

[33] For an explanation, see CRS Report R42024, *Oil Price Fluctuations*, by Neelesh Nerurkar and Mark Jickling.

[34] Robert McNally, *Managing Oil Market Disruption in a Confrontation with Iran*, Council on Foreign Relations, January 2012.

[35] Humeyra Pamuk and Dmitry Zhdannikov, "UAE Delays Oil Pipeline to Bypass Hormuz," *Reuters*, January 9, 2012.

---

A disruption of oil through the Strait of Hormuz could significantly affect global oil prices. Though most of the flows through the Strait go to Asia, the oil market is globally integrated and a disruption anywhere can contribute to higher oil prices everywhere. A disruption of oil exported from the Persian Gulf to Asia would leave Asian refineries bidding for oil from alternative sources elsewhere. Due to the wide number of relevant variables, there is significant uncertainty on how much a disruption could contribute to higher crude oil prices. While disruption risks in the past may have contributed to prices being higher than they might have otherwise been, actual Iran-related events have not necessarily resulted in clear and significant price increases ex-post (see **Table 1**). The numerous variables affecting the price of oil at any given time can make it difficult to estimate what specific change in price is due to a specific event. Nonetheless, reductions or threatened reductions to supply do tend to push oil prices up.

Key uncertainties for the impact of a disruption would be how much global oil supply was reduced, risks of further reductions, and duration of the disruption. Risk of damage to oil production and export facilities in the Persian Gulf would also be of concern. The response of oil-importing countries would also be important, namely if and how consumer countries released strategic oil stockpiles, in addition to any possible military response. Conditions in the rest of the oil market and the global economy would also affect how prices eventually responded. For example, disruptions that occur during periods of strong global oil demand growth and limited supply growth elsewhere may have a relatively greater price impacts than those that occur when demand is falling and other sources of supply are growing or commercial oil inventories are high.

Given limited bypass options, outright closure of the Strait would represent an unprecedented disruption to global oil supply and would likely cause a substantial increase in oil prices. However, as suggested above, outright closure may be unlikely, and even if it occurred, might not persist for very long. Another possibility is the harassment of tanker traffic through the Strait as described above. The impact of harassment would depend on the degree to which it effectively reduced oil exports through the Strait and its duration. Harassment could reduce the rate at which oil exited the Gulf, raise the cost of transport, and raise worries of future disruption. A third possibility—one already pursued by Iran—is that Iranian officials can make threatening statements suggesting they will disrupt tanker traffic. The increased perception of risk could contribute to higher oil prices without requiring military action, though this is only effective in contributing to oil prices as long as and to the degree that global oil market participants take such threats seriously. Such a measure can benefit Iran by increasing their oil revenues without risking military retaliation.

In the event of a disruption, consumer countries could release strategic stocks to offset the impact on oil supply. The United States currently holds 696 million barrels of crude oil in the Strategic Petroleum Reserve (SPR),[36] a publicly held stockpile of crude oil to be used to offset supply disruptions.[37] The United States coordinates use of its SPR with other members of the International Energy Agency (IEA), which include Japan, Germany, South Korea, and other members of the Organization for Economic Cooperation and Development (OECD). Oil importing members of the IEA have an obligation to hold oil stocks equal to at least 90 days worth of net imports. The IEA has coordinated to collectively release stocks three times since the

---

[36] Energy Information Administration, *Stocks by Type*, December 29, 2011, http://www.eia.gov/dnav/pet/pet_stoc_typ_d_nus_SAS_mbbl_m htm.

[37] For more background the SPR, see CRS Report R41687, *The Strategic Petroleum Reserve and Refined Product Reserves: Authorization and Drawdown Policy*, by Anthony Andrews and Robert Pirog

organization was created in the wake of the 1973/1974 oil crisis: after Iraq's invasion of Kuwait in 1990/1991; after Hurricanes Katrina and Rita in 2005; and in response to prolonged disruption of Libyan oil production in 2011. IEA countries hold about 4.2 billion barrels of crude oil and refined products in inventory, of which 1.5 billion are held by governments.[38] If drawn down at the maximum rate technically possible, these government-held stocks could be delivered to the market at an average rate of 10.4 Mb/d of crude oil and 4 Mb/d of products in the first month of an IEA collective action, diminishing thereafter.[39] (The rate diminishes as stocks are depleted.) By offsetting the loss of supply, a strategic stock release could blunt the impact a disruption can have on oil prices.

There are several additional resources to respond to an oil supply emergency. In some IEA member countries oil companies are required by governments to hold emergency stocks. These can be made available to supplement a release government held strategic stocks elsewhere. IEA members can also coordinate demand restraint measures to offset the impact of a supply disruption.[40] Some non-OECD governments, including China, have started building strategic stocks and some oil exporters, including Saudi Arabia, hold small amounts of crude in storage near consumer markets.[41]

## Conclusion

Concerns about broadening international sanctions on Iran's oil exports prompted some Iranian officials to make threatening statements about closing the Strait of Hormuz. Iran has invested in the military capability to close or disrupt traffic through the Strait. If Iran attempted to do so, the United States—which has invested in military preparedness to keep the Strait open—would respond, potentially joined by other countries. Such a military response may or may not be limited to simply reopening the Strait for transit.

The threat of military response, coupled with its economic concern about disrupting commerce with its own trading partners, makes Iran unlikely to attempt to close the Strait of Hormuz. Iran has the option of harassing tanker traffic through the Gulf as it has in the past, though that also runs the risk of military retaliation and alienating customers. However, it is possible that Iranian action becomes relatively more likely as more countries reduce or refuse Iranian exports. Alternatively, Iran may choose to continue making threatening statements without actually acting and/or to seek a diplomatic solution to curb oil sanctions through renewing international talks on its nuclear program. A disruption of oil exports through the Strait would have significant impacts on oil prices around the world. To some degree a disruption could be offset by release from the U.S. Strategic Petroleum Reserve and similar reserves in other countries. Even without an extant

---

[38] International Energy Agency, *Oil Market Report*, December 13, 2011, p. 68, http://omrpublic.iea.org/currentissues/full.pdf. The remaining inventories are held by companies either for purely commercial reasons or as required by their governments to maintain enough stocks to meet their IEA commitment.

[39] International Energy Agency, *Fact Sheet: IEA Stocks and Drawdown Capacity*, February 25, 2011, http://www.iea.org/files/Potential_IEA_Stockdraw_Capacity.pdf.

[40] International Energy Agency, *IEA Response System for Oil Supply Emergencies, 2011*, 2011, p. 10, http://www.iea.org/publications/free_new_Desc.asp?PUBS_ID=1912.

[41] Aramco and the Abu Dhabi National Oil Company have storage facilities for commercial and emergency use in Japan, leased for free in return for prioritizing emergency supplies to Japan if they become necessary. Aramco also has some storage in the Netherlands. Aramco had leased 5 million barrels of storage capacity in St. Eustacia in the Caribbean but relinquished it in 2009.

disruption, concerns about a future disruption may also contribute to oil prices being higher than they might otherwise be by creating uncertainty about a large portion of the world's oil supply. Iran has the option of making threatening statements about the Strait without actually acting, which is what it has been doing since December 2011. So long as oil market participants consider this a credible future threat, it could contribute to upward pressure on oil prices.

Even prior to Iran's recent threats, legislation in Congress to increase sanctions on Iran was pending, and some had been recently adopted, such as sanctions against banks that do business with Iran's Central Bank. Some legislation still pending might receive more attention in light of Iran's threats to the Strait. If hostilities with Iran were to occur in the Strait, it is likely that the question of presidential authority to use force will be raised.

## Table 1. Selected Iran-Related Events and Oil Price Changes

| Event | Price Changes | | Commentary |
|---|---|---|---|
| | **Prior Month** | **Next Month** | |
| *Start of Iran/Iraq War, 9/23/1980[a]* | 0.1% | 0.5% | The monthly oil price did not change much prior to this conflict beginning and even a month into it. However, six months into the conflict oil prices were up 11%. |
| *"Tanker War" begins, 3/27/1984* | -0.2% | -0.9% | The "tanker war" included 44 attacks against tankers from other nations over the course of nine months. During this time, prices remained close to the March 27 price or lower, dropping 14% by the end of the period. The large drop is more reflective of the global oil market than the uncertainty created by the tanker war. Supply levels remained high during the time period, while demand was growing slowly.[b] |
| *Re-flagged Bridgeton hits a mine (Operation Earnest Will), 7/24/1987* | 0.4% | -9.6% | The Bridgeton, carrying the U.S. flag, hit a mine in the Persian Gulf. Under U.S. Operation Earnest Will, ships of Kuwaiti tankers were re-flagged with the U.S. flag so that the U.S. Navy could protect them in the Persian Gulf. Prices stayed above the July 24th price for almost three weeks before steadily declining. As minimal oil was interrupted overall, the risk to supply was decreased consequently putting downward pressure on prices.[c] |
| *Operation Praying Mantis, 4/18/1988* | 11.7% | -5.9% | The operation destroyed almost 40% of Iran's navy. Prices after the event dropped immediately with the biggest daily drop almost 5% two weeks later. Praying Mantis greatly diminished Iran's capabilities in the Persian Gulf, decreasing the likelihood of an oil cutoff. Leading up to U.S. Operation Praying Mantis, the overall oil market faced lower demand because of warm weather in Europe, and higher production as Saudi Arabia was producing at its OPEC quota and no longer below it and non-OPEC production was higher than it had been.[d] |
| *Iran arms Strait of Hormuz, 3/28/1995* | 3.0% | 3.0% | The Pentagon announced that it was monitoring Iranian installation of missiles in the Strait of Hormuz. Iran also took possession and fortified two nearby islands claimed by them and the United Arab Emirates. During the month after the announcement daily prices fluctuated up and down before jumping at the end of the period. However, about a week after the event began prices declined eight consecutive days. |
| *Iran threatens the Strait, 12/28/2011* | 1.2% | -0.4% | Iran's first Vice President Mohammad Reza Rahimi was the first to threaten closure of the Strait. Prices initially rose almost daily from this event, peaking on January 4, almost 4% higher before declining. |

**Source:** U.S. Energy Information Administration, Annual Oil Market Chronology, http://www.eia.gov/emeu/cabs/AOMC/8089.html.

**Notes:** Crude prices are NYMEX West Texas Intermediate crude prices (daily) except 1980, which is refiners acquisition cost of crude reported by EIA (monthly).

a.   Although there were events leading up to September 23, 1980 that contributed to hostilities, this date is used as a start date to the military conflict.

b.   U.S. Energy Information Administration (EIA), *Short-Term Energy Outlook*, DOE/EIA-0202(84/3Q), Washington, DC, August 1984, p. 12, http://www.eia.gov/forecasts/steo/archives/3Q84.pdf.

c.   EIA, *Short-Term Energy Outlook*, DOE/EIA-0202(87/4Q), Washington, DC, October 1987, p. 9, http://www.eia.gov/forecasts/steo/archives/4Q87.pdf.

d.   EIA, *Short-Term Energy Outlook*, DOE/EIA-0202(88/2Q), Washington, DC, April 1988, p. 7, http://www.eia.gov/forecasts/steo/archives/2Q88.pdf.

# Appendix A. Legal Framework Applicable to International Straits

A "global diplomatic effort to regulate and write rules for all ocean areas, all uses of the seas and all of its resources" led the United Nations to convene the Third United Nations Conference on the Sea in 1973[42] and adoption of the United Nations Convention on the Law of the Sea (UNCLOS) in 1982.[43] The Convention states:

> *Recognizing* the desirability of establishing through this Convention, with due regard for the sovereignty of all States, a legal order for the seas and oceans which will facilitate international communication, and will promote the peaceful uses of the seas and oceans ... *Believing* that the codification and progressive development of the law of the sea achieved in this Convention will contribute to the strengthening of peace, security, cooperation and friendly relations among all nations in conformity with the principles of justice and equal rights ... [and] *Affirming* that matters not regulated by this Convention continue to be governed by the rules and principles of general international law...

Parties to the Convention agreed to the adoption of the comprehensive international treaty after nine years of negotiations. UNCLOS generally incorporates the rules of international law codified in the 1958 United Nations Convention on the High Seas,[44] but also comprehensively addresses the use of other areas of the sea including, for example, the territorial seas, natural resources, and the seabed. While the United States is a signatory to the 1958 Convention on the High Seas, it is not a party to UNCLOS. However, UNCLOS is generally viewed as a codification of customary international law.[45] With respect to the coastal nations bordering the Straits of Hormuz, Iran is a signatory to UNCLOS [46] but has not ratified the Convention and Oman is both a signatory to and has ratified the Convention.[47]

---

[42] The United Nations Convention on the Law of the Sea (A historical perspective), available at http://www.un.org/ Depts/los/convention_agreements/convention_historical_perspective htm.

[43] United Nations Convention on the Law of the Seas (UNCLOS), 21 I.L.M. 1261. Convention adopted December 10, 1982. Entered into force November 16, 1994 (the United States is not a party to the Agreement).

[44] Convention on the High Seas, 13 U.S.T. 2312; T.I.A.S. 5200; 450 U.N.T.S. 82. Signed at Geneva, April 29, 1958. Entered into force September 30, 1962.

[45] *See* Presidential Proclamation 5030, President Ronald Reagan, March 10, 1983 *available* at http://www.state.gov/ documents/organization/58381.pdf. For a discussion on policy issues related to ratification of UNCLOS, *see* CRS Report RS21890, *The U.N. Law of the Sea Convention and the United States: Developments Since October 2003*, by Marjorie Ann Browne.

[46] The Islamic Republic of Iran signed the Convention on 10 December 1982, with the following declaration, in part:
> In accordance with article 310 of the Convention on the Law of the Sea, the Government of the Islamic Republic of Iran seizes the opportunity at this solemn moment of signing the Convention, to place on the records its "understanding" in relation to certain provisions of the Convention. The main objective for submitting these declarations is the avoidance of eventual future interpretation of the following articles in a manner incompatible with the original intention and previous positions or in disharmony with national laws and regulations of the Islamic Republic of Iran. It is ... the understanding of the Islamic Republic of Iran that:

> 1) Notwithstanding the intended character of the Convention being one of general application and of law making nature, certain of its provisions are merely product of quid pro quo which do not necessarily purport to codify the existing customs or established usage (practice) regarded as having an obligatory character. Therefore, it seems natural and in harmony with article 34 of the 1969 Vienna Convention on the Law of Treaties, that only states parties to the Law of the Sea

(continued...)

Straits used for international navigation are addressed in UNCLOS. Specifically, Part III (Arts. 34-45) of the Convention is comprised of various provisions related to the legal status of waters forming straits and authorized forms of passage through such waters. The general provisions (Arts. 34-36) establish the legal status of waters forming straits and scope of application.[48] The remaining Articles in Part III identify the legal regimes of transit passage and innocent passage, including the rights and duties of transiting vessels as well as the rights and duties of States bordering the straits.

Transit passage is defined as "the exercise in accordance with this Part of the freedom of navigation and overflight solely for the purpose of continuous and expeditious transit of the strait between one part of the high seas or an exclusive economic zone and another part of the high seas or an exclusive economic zone."[49] While exercising the right of transit passage, ships and aircraft are required to: (a) proceed without delay through or over the strait; (b) refrain from any threat or use of force against the sovereignty, territorial integrity or political independence of the States bordering the strait; and (c) refrain from any activities other than those incident to their normal modes of continuous and expeditious transit unless necessary by *force majeure* or by distress.[50] The States bordering the straits may adopt laws and regulations related to safety and navigation of maritime traffic, pollution, fishing, and commodity trades.[51] However, authorized laws and regulations "shall not discriminate in form or in fact among foreign ships or in their application have the practical effect of denying, hampering or impairing the right of transit passage."[52]

In support of the safety and navigation of maritime traffic, States bordering straits may "designate sea lanes and prescribe traffic separation schemes ... to promote the safe passage of ships."[53] With respect to the Straits of Hormuz, the States bordering the straits have designated sea lanes and a traffic separation scheme as adopted by the Maritime Safety Committee of the Inter-Governmental Maritime Consultative Organization (a specialized agency of the United Nations,

---

(...continued)

    Convention shall be entitled to benefit from the contractual rights created therein.

    The above considerations pertain specifically (but not exclusively) to the following:

      -- The right of Transit passage through straits used for international navigation (Part III, Section 2, article 38).

      -- The notion of "Exclusive Economic Zone" (Part V). - All matters regarding the International Seabed Area and the Concept of "Common Heritage of mankind" (Part XI)." Available at http://www.un.org/depts/los/convention_agreements/convention_declarations.htm.

[47] Oman signed the Convention on July 1, 1983 with the following declaration: "It is the understanding of the Government of the Sultanate of Oman that the application of the provisions of articles 19, 25, 34, 38 and 45 of the Convention does not preclude a coastal State from taking such appropriate measures as are necessary to protect its interest of peace and security." Oman ratified the Convention on August 17, 1989 with an additional seven declarations. Available at http://www.un.org/depts/los/convention_agreements/convention_declarations.htm.

[48] UNCLOS, Article 34 – Legal status of waters forming straits used for international navigation; UNCLOS, Article 35 – Scope of this Part; and UNCLOS Article 36 – High seas routes or routes through exclusive economic zones through straits used for international navigation.

[49] Ibid. at Art. 38, Para. 2.

[50] Ibid. at Art. 39, Para. 1. *See also* Department of the Navy, Office of the Chief of Naval Operations and Headquarters, U.S. Marine Corps, Department of Homeland Security and U.S. Coast Guard, *The Commander's Handbook on the Law of Naval Operations*, NWP 1-14M, MCWP 5-12.1, COMDTPUB P5800.7A, Para. 2.5.3.1, July 2007.

[51] UNCLOS, Art. 42, Para. 1.

[52] Ibid. at Art. 43, Para. 2.

[53] Ibid. at Art. 41, Para. 1.

---

now known as the International Maritime Organization (IMO)) in 1979.[54] States bordering straits may substitute other sea lanes or traffic separation schemes, after consultation with a competent international organization (IMO).[55] Ships in transit passage are required to respect the applicable sea lanes and traffic separation schemes established in accordance with UNCLOS.[56] Finally, States bordering straits "shall not hamper transit passage and shall give appropriate publicity to any danger to navigation or overflight within or over the strait of which they have knowledge. There shall be no suspension of transit passage."[57]

# Author Contact Information

Kenneth Katzman, Coordinator
Specialist in Middle Eastern Affairs
kkatzman@crs.loc.gov, 7-7612

Neelesh Nerurkar, Coordinator
Specialist in Energy Policy
nnerurkar@crs.loc.gov, 7-2873

Ronald O'Rourke
Specialist in Naval Affairs
rorourke@crs.loc.gov, 7-7610

R. Chuck Mason
Legislative Attorney
rcmason@crs.loc.gov, 7-9294

Michael Ratner
Specialist in Energy Policy
mratner@crs.loc.gov, 7-9529

---

[54] See U.S. Department of Homeland Security, United States Coast Guard, Navigation Center available at http://navcen.uscg.gov/pdf/imo/COLREGSCirculars/COLREG2-Circ11.pdf.

[55] UNCLOS, Art. 41, Paras. 2 & 4.

[56] *Id.* at Art. 41, Para. 7.

[57] *Id.* at Art. 44.

www.ingramcontent.com/pod-product-compliance
Lightning Source LLC
Chambersburg PA
CBHW082207290526

45794CB00008B/3452